DISABILITIES CAN'T STOP US!

FRANKLIN D. ROOSEVELT

More Important than Fear

Therese M. Shea

PowerKiDS press.
New York

Published in 2021 by The Rosen Publishing Group, Inc.
29 East 21st Street, New York, NY 10010

First Edition

Editor: Amanda Vink
Book Design: Reann Nye

Photo Credits: Series art (letter) Arkady Mazor/Shutterstock.com; series art (background) Ratana21/Shutterstock.com; cover George Skadding/The LIFE Picture Collection/Getty Images; p. 5 Hulton Archive/Getty Images; p. 7 Stock Montage/Archive Photos/Getty Images; p. 9 Library of Congress/Corbis Historical/Getty Images; pp. 11, 17 PhotoQuest/Archive Photos/Getty Images; pp. 13, 15 New York Daily News Archive/New York Daily News/Getty Images; pp. 19, 21, 23, 29 Bettmann/Getty Images; p. 25 FPG/Archive Photos/Getty Images; p. 27 Historical/ Corbis Historical/Getty Images.

Library of Congress Cataloging-in-Publication Data
Names: Shea, Therese, author.
Title: Franklin D. Roosevelt : more important than fear / Therese M. Shea.
Other titles: More important than fear
Description: New York : PowerKids Press, [2021] | Series: Disabilities can't stop us! | Includes bibliographical references and index. | Summary: "Franklin D. Roosevelt was the president who led the nation out of the Great Depression and during most of World War II. He was also a polio survivor! Though the disease left his legs paralyzed, he refused to let that stop his ambitions. Readers will be fascinated by this lesser-known part of FDR's life as well as by the efforts he made to help others with polio. Sidebars add more information about this extraordinary man's life, while historical photographs help young history lovers better understand the time period."- Provided by publisher.
Identifiers: LCCN 2019037561 | ISBN 9781725311282 (library binding) | ISBN 9781725311268 (paperback) | ISBN 9781725311275 |
Subjects: LCSH: Roosevelt, Franklin D. (Franklin Delano), 1882-1945–Juvenile literature. | Presidents–United States–Biography–Juvenile literature. | People with disabilities–United States–Biography–Juvenile literature. | United States–Politics and government–1933-1945–Juvenile literature.
Classification: LCC E807 .S427 2021 | DDC 973.917092 [B]–dc23
LC record available at https://lccn.loc.gov/2019037561

Manufactured in the United States of America

CPSIA Compliance Information: Batch #CSPK20: For Further Information contact Rosen Publishing, New York, New York at 1-800-237-9932

CONTENTS

FDR

Franklin D. Roosevelt, often known as FDR, is among the most famous presidents of the United States. He was the only president to have been elected four times. He steered the country through the long period of economic troubles called the Great Depression. He led the United States through most of World War II as well.

Through these hard times, this powerful leader was living with a physical disability. He was partially **paralyzed** after he survived an illness at the age of 39. Afterward, Roosevelt was permanently disabled. He needed help to walk, using **crutches**, braces, and the assistance of others for the rest of his life. In this book, you'll learn how FDR coped with his disability and became the president the United States needed in its darkest times.

FDR's disability didn't stop him from pursuing his dreams. >

FDR on Facing Fear

After FDR was sworn in as president for the first time, he gave a speech in which he said: "The only thing we have to fear is fear itself—nameless, unreasoning, unjustified terror which paralyzes needed efforts to convert retreat into advance." In his personal life, Roosevelt had to face his own fear about entering public life again after his paralysis. He rejected this fear and advanced personally, physically, and professionally to the nation's highest office.

Getting into Politics

Franklin Delano Roosevelt was born January 30, 1882, in Hyde Park, New York. He was the only child in a wealthy family. He was educated at home until he was 14 years old, when he began to attend Groton Preparatory School in Groton, Massachusetts. In 1900, he started his studies at Harvard University. During his time in college, Roosevelt met his future wife, Eleanor Roosevelt, who was a distant cousin and the niece of President Theodore Roosevelt. Eleanor and Franklin Roosevelt married in 1905.

After Harvard, Roosevelt attended law school at Columbia University. However, he wasn't very interested in law. Roosevelt ran for New York State Senate in 1910. He ran as a Democrat and surprised many people by winning the election in a largely Republican district.

UNSTOPPABLE!

At Groton, FDR grew to admire the career of his cousin Theodore Roosevelt, who was president from 1901 to 1909.

Although the odds seemed against him, FDR campaigned hard for a state senate seat in 1910—and won.

Life Changes

During Roosevelt's second term as a state senator, President Woodrow Wilson appointed him to be assistant secretary of the U.S. Navy. Roosevelt prepared the navy to enter World War I in 1917. In 1920, the Democratic Party asked him to run for vice president, with James Cox as the presidential candidate. Though Republican Warren Harding won the presidency, Roosevelt became well known in national politics.

However, in 1921, while on vacation at Campobello Island in New Brunswick, Canada, Roosevelt fell ill. He became feverish and weak. First, he lost feeling in his left leg. A day later, he was paralyzed from the stomach down and in great pain. Doctors weren't sure what was wrong with him.

UNSTOPPABLE!

As a state senator, FDR earned a reputation for fighting against dishonest practices in politics, such as those of the New York City political organization Tammany Hall.

James Cox

FDR

Though his vice presidential campaign was unsuccessful, FDR was a likable candidate. People talked about his **charisma**.

The Diagnosis

Finally, in August 1921, Dr. Robert Lovett **diagnosed** FDR's illness as the disease called infantile paralysis or poliomyelitis (polio). Polio, which is caused by a virus, usually affected young children. In fact, children who didn't fall ill from polio usually developed immunity, or resistance, to it. Roosevelt had not. He had been a sickly child, so some thought his immune system had never been able to fight it completely. Additionally, his last few years in politics had been stressful ones, further compromising his immune system.

Even after FDR was no longer sick, the road to full recovery was long. He wanted to exercise to regain use of his muscles. However, for weeks he was only allowed to sit up in a chair an hour each day.

In fall 1921, Franklin Roosevelt left the hospital and returned to his home in New York City. >

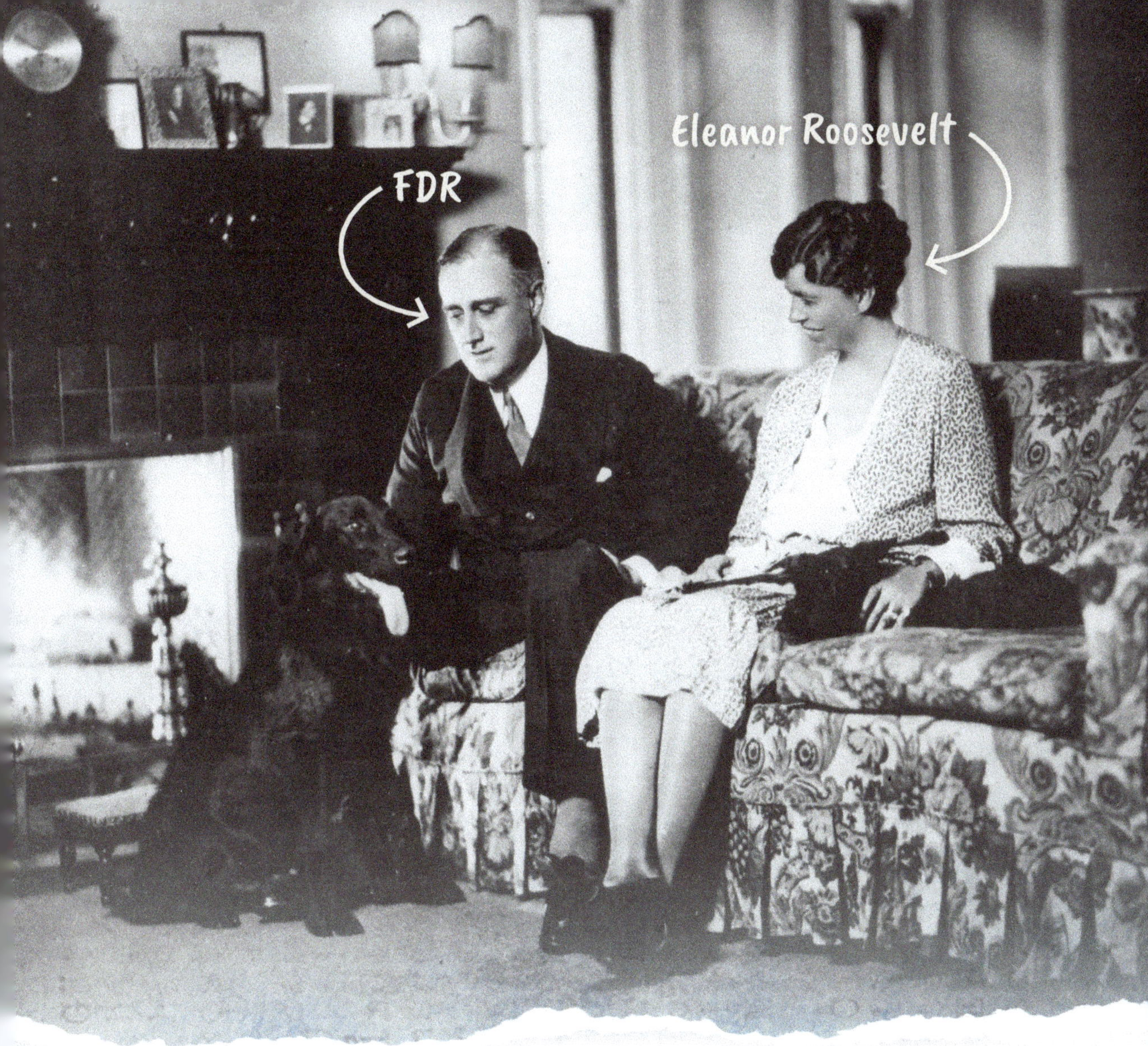

What Is Polio?

Polio usually causes mild illness or no obvious illness at all. However, in some people, it can lead to paralysis or even death. The virus spreads through exposure to the bodily waste of an infected person. FDR developed the illness before doctors created polio vaccines in the 1950s. In recent years, some scientists have rediagnosed FDR with the nervous system disorder Guillain-Barré syndrome, mainly because of his age when he became ill. However, others think this diagnosis isn't likely.

His Fight to Recover

By December 1921, the virus was gone from Roosevelt's body, but no one knew how much muscle function he would regain. Some nerve cells had been destroyed forever, but other cells could recover with the right treatment. A nurse helped him exercise his stomach and lower back, and those areas made a full recovery. This allowed FDR to begin doing pull-ups. His upper body became very strong.

However, Roosevelt made the mistake of pushing himself too much too soon, which caused him great pain. He was in a body cast for two weeks to straighten his legs. Finally, in February 1922, he was allowed to get on his feet for the first time in months. His leg muscles weren't strong enough to hold him. He needed braces.

For the rest of his life, FDR was devoted to exercise. Swimming was a favorite sport of his because his legs could support his upper body more easily in the water.

Life with Braces

FDR's braces were specially fitted to his legs. Each weighed 13 pounds (5.9 kg)! When the braces were locked, they held his body in a standing position. He then used crutches to help him move. Even with these aids, Roosevelt fell many times as he learned to walk again. His first set of braces proved to be too **flexible**, bending under the weight of his body. Doctors created a sturdier pair that performed better. However, he never really got used to braces and often didn't wear them.

Roosevelt worked with a woman named Wilhelmine Wright, who taught him tricks to help him move. He learned to stand with his braces, walk with crutches, and go up and down stairs.

UNSTOPPABLE!

One of FDR's goals was to walk ¼ mile (0.4 km) down the driveway at his home in Hyde Park, New York. While he never achieved this, he reached many other goals.

In this photo, FDR makes his way downstairs. You can see his braces near his feet.

Family and Friends

FDR gained **confidence** as he learned to navigate the world in new ways. He continued to try to exceed his doctors' expectations. His relationship with his family changed, too. Though his children feared for his health at first, they grew to accept what had happened and aided him when he needed it. Eleanor said, "The perfect naturalness with which the children accepted [FDR's] limitations though they had always known him as an active person, helped him tremendously in his own acceptance of them."

FDR liked to have friends and family around him as he exercised. Laughing and having cheerful conversations took his mind off what he was doing. In fact, some of FDR's closest relationships developed during that hard time in his life.

FDR's son James sometimes acted as his aide as he stood and moved around in public.

James Roosevelt
FDR

Warm Springs

In the western part of the state of Georgia, water flows from the side of Pine Mountain and creates warm springs. Because of these pools of water, people gave the nearby town the name "Warm Springs." A resort in which people could bathe in the springs had the same name. In 1923, a friend told Franklin Roosevelt that a young polio patient had bathed in the waters and recovered. Curious, Roosevelt visited the next year.

Though the waters didn't cure FDR, he did believe they helped him move one of his legs. In 1926, he bought the resort. The next year, he established the Warm Springs Foundation and gave this property to the organization. The foundation created the only hospital in the United States devoted to treating people with polio at that time.

At Warm Springs, FDR enjoyed meeting other people who had suffered from polio.

The Little White House

FDR continued to visit Warm Springs in the years that followed. When he could, he met with patients there to share experiences and take a swim. He had Thanksgiving dinner there as well. Roosevelt had a house built at Warm Springs that later became known as the Little White House. He died in that house in 1945. The home looks just as it did that day. Visitors can tour this historic site.

Back to Political Life

By 1924, it became clear that no matter how much FDR exercised, he would never walk without help. He had to make a decision: go back to his political life as he was or give up his career. Eleanor and his friend Louis Howe encouraged him to return to public life. Roosevelt was concerned about how people might view him. At that time, people with disabilities often weren't treated with respect. In fact, many were placed in **institutions** away from others.

On June 26, 1924, FDR spoke at the Democratic National Convention in New York City in support of New York governor Al Smith, who was running for president. Roosevelt moved to the **podium** using two crutches. The movement was hard for him, but the political rewards of the speech were great.

UNSTOPPABLE!

One person asked FDR to retire from public life—his mother. She thought he should protect his health by staying away from a stressful political career.

The more time FDR spent in public, the more he felt accepted and ready to resume his political career.

Governor Roosevelt

Al Smith suggested that FDR run for governor of New York in 1928. As Roosevelt campaigned, many people saw him as an **optimistic** and energetic man—but also one who understood life's hardships. However, opponents tried to use his disability against him. Smith answered back on FDR's behalf: "A governor does not have to be an acrobat. We do not elect him for his ability to do a double backflip or a handspring." Roosevelt won the election.

When the nation entered the Great Depression in 1929, Roosevelt supported plans that assisted New Yorkers who lost their jobs and were struggling to survive. People appreciated his programs so much that he was reelected to another term. Many people also viewed him as a strong candidate for president.

FDR sometimes campaigned from the back of an open car. Here, he's pictured next to his daughter, Anna, and his wife, Eleanor.

The Great Depression

The Great Depression was the worst economic period ever in the United States and the world. It lasted about 10 years. People who'd invested in stocks lost a lot of money. Many lost trust in banks and tried to remove all their money, causing banks to fail. About 15 million people were out of work at one point. At the same time, a **drought** in the middle of the country caused farms to fail. Never had so many Americans been so poor.

President Roosevelt

FDR's disability wasn't an issue for most people when he decided to run for president. Again, his political opponents tried to make it an issue. In 1931, a magazine ran a story titled "Is Franklin D. Roosevelt Physically Fit to Be President?" It stated: "The next President of the United States may be a **cripple**." Still, FDR was chosen as the Democratic Party's candidate for president.

Americans were interested in one election issue in 1932: how to recover from the Great Depression. Herbert Hoover, the sitting president, received blame for not doing enough to help people. Meanwhile, Roosevelt promised to put programs in place that would help those who were suffering. Roosevelt received about 7 million votes more than Hoover. The **Electoral College** vote was 472 for Roosevelt and 59 for Hoover.

UNSTOPPABLE!

Roosevelt's plan for economic recovery was called the New Deal. While some didn't like that he expanded the powers of the federal government for these programs, others welcomed any relief.

During the first 100 days of his term, FDR put many programs in place to tackle the Great Depression. While they didn't stop the depression, Americans felt more hopeful about the future.

The President in Private

Roosevelt was elected president three more times. He boldly led the United States into World War II after Japan bombed Pearl Harbor, Hawaii, in 1941. While FDR used crutches and braces in his public life, he often used a wheelchair to move around at home. He had a chair specially made from a dining chair, which could be wheeled around corners more easily than the large wheelchairs of that time.

In public, though, Roosevelt liked to stand and give the appearance of being able to walk. To do this, he often used a cane on one side of his body and the arm of someone on his other side for support. Then, he'd move his hips and legs forward, pushing forward his whole body.

The president asked photographers and members of the press to avoid taking pictures of him dealing with his disability. One of FDR's special wheelchairs is seen here at his home in Hyde Park, New York.

The March of Dimes

In 1938, FDR founded an organization close to his heart—the National Foundation for Infantile Paralysis. The "March of Dimes" campaign for this organization urged radio listeners to send dimes to the White House to raise funds for polio research. The money helped fund studies that led to the polio vaccine. In 1979, the organization changed its name to the March of Dimes Foundation. It works today to prevent childhood diseases and disorders and support other causes.

Through the War

In March 1945, after attending an important meeting with world leaders, FDR addressed Congress. For the first time in public, he was pushed in a wheelchair. He said, "I hope that you will pardon me for this unusual **posture** of sitting down, but I know that you will realize that it makes it a lot easier for me not to have to carry about 10 pounds of steel around on the bottom of my legs."

In April 1945, FDR, who suffered from heart disease, visited the Little White House in Warm Springs. He died there on April 12. The nation mourned. As the years passed, people remembered FDR not for his disability but for his powerful leadership during the country's hardest times.

This image of FDR in the Oval Office was the last color photograph taken before his death. >

FDR Memorial

One of the statues at the Franklin Delano Roosevelt Memorial in Washington, DC, shows FDR sitting in a wheelchair. While Roosevelt rarely showed the true degree of his disability in public, planners decided that this statue would show the man as he truly was to inspire others with disabilities. He once said: "I am a symbol of what can happen when people with disabilities are strongly supported." FDR likely would have supported this statue and the reasoning behind it.

TIMELINE

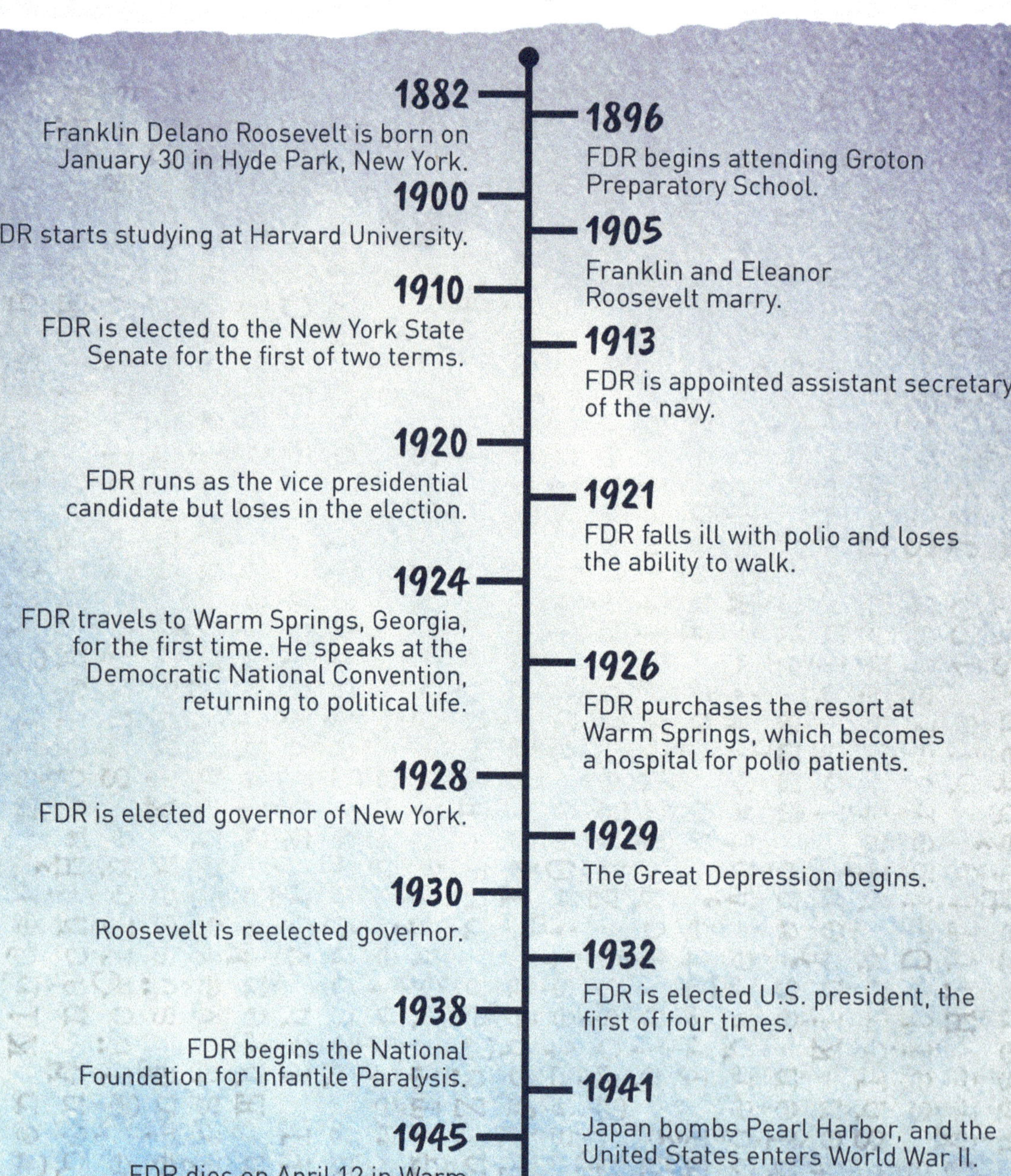

1882
Franklin Delano Roosevelt is born on January 30 in Hyde Park, New York.

1896
FDR begins attending Groton Preparatory School.

1900
FDR starts studying at Harvard University.

1905
Franklin and Eleanor Roosevelt marry.

1910
FDR is elected to the New York State Senate for the first of two terms.

1913
FDR is appointed assistant secretary of the navy.

1920
FDR runs as the vice presidential candidate but loses in the election.

1921
FDR falls ill with polio and loses the ability to walk.

1924
FDR travels to Warm Springs, Georgia, for the first time. He speaks at the Democratic National Convention, returning to political life.

1926
FDR purchases the resort at Warm Springs, which becomes a hospital for polio patients.

1928
FDR is elected governor of New York.

1929
The Great Depression begins.

1930
Roosevelt is reelected governor.

1932
FDR is elected U.S. president, the first of four times.

1938
FDR begins the National Foundation for Infantile Paralysis.

1941
Japan bombs Pearl Harbor, and the United States enters World War II.

1945
FDR dies on April 12 in Warm Springs, Georgia.

GLOSSARY

charisma: An appeal that causes people to feel excited about someone.

confidence: A feeling or belief that you can do something well or succeed at something.

cripple: An offensive term for a person who cannot move or walk normally because of a permanent injury or other problem.

crutch: A long stick with a padded piece at the top that fits under an arm.

diagnose: To identify a disease by its signs and symptoms.

drought: A period of time during which there is very little or no rain.

Electoral College: A body of electors who cast votes to elect the president and vice president.

flexible: Able to bend easily.

institution: A place where a group takes care of a person, usually for a long period of time.

optimistic: Having or showing hope for the future.

paralyzed: Unable to move.

podium: A stand with a surface that holds a book or notes for someone who is speaking.

posture: The way your body is positioned when you are sitting or standing.

INDEX

WEBSITES

Due to the changing nature of Internet links, PowerKids Press has developed an online list of websites related to the subject of this book. This site is updated regularly. Please use this link to access the list: www.powerkidslinks.com/dcsu/roosevelt